# Meditations on an Empty Stomach

*poems by*

# Michael Lee Bross

*Finishing Line Press*
Georgetown, Kentucky

# Meditations on an Empty Stomach

Copyright © 2019 by Michael Lee Bross
ISBN 978-1-64662-054-8  First Edition
All rights reserved under International and Pan-American Copyright Conventions. No part of this book may be reproduced in any manner whatsoever without written permission from the publisher, except in the case of brief quotations embodied in critical articles and reviews.

## ACKNOWLEDGMENTS

Previous editions of "Playground Metaphor" and "First Steps" previously appeared on *Let's Talk Philadelphia*, September 15th, 2016

Publisher: Leah Maines
Editor: Christen Kincaid
Cover Art: Amanda Quevedo
Author Photo: Adrienne Bross
Cover Design: Elizabeth Maines McCleavy

Printed in the USA on acid-free paper.
Order online: www.finishinglinepress.com
        also available on amazon.com

        Author inquiries and mail orders:
              Finishing Line Press
                P. O. Box 1626
            Georgetown, Kentucky 40324
                   U. S. A.

# Table of Contents

First Steps ................................................................ 1

Delivery Room ........................................................ 2

Meditation on an Empty Stomach ...................... 3

Baby Food ................................................................ 4

Questions for Babies ............................................. 5

On teaching my daughter proper nutrition ...... 6

Meditation on an Empty Stomach ...................... 7

Still Life of a Candy Apple .................................... 8

A Playground Metaphor ....................................... 9

Meditation on an Empty Stomach .................... 10

Falling Asleep to Berryman and my Daughter's Lullaby ............... 11

Stranger Danger .................................................. 12

The End of Play .................................................... 13

Meditation on an Empty Stomach .................... 14

Parental Advice ................................................... 15

Practice to Write ................................................. 16

Explaining Bombs to Babies .............................. 18

Colic ...................................................................... 20

Baby Talk .............................................................. 21

Learning to Cook ................................................. 22

Meditation on an Empty Stomach .................... 23

My Gratitude ....................................................... 24

*To Ariadne:*
*For showing me what the world looks like*
*before we are told how to look at it*

**First Steps**

We all teeter on the lip of tragedy,
tethering the balance with which we manage this world
like a broken kite spun by the mercy of the wind

now shake each foot in the presence of ground and gravity

that pulls us into the dirt
or casts us out without notice

so on impact baby,
may we crack the earth
rise and cry in the face of calamity
and in the same direction
stumble towards joy.

**Delivery Room**

Your face inflates
from your mother's vagina like a wet rubber
glove, a viscous and screaming prune,
nurses toweling birth canal streaks from your cheeks.
I know this confusion of fluids,
with what organ pilots that tickle in the pit of your gut,
now a confusion
of how I hold your mother
with you in the room,
how my cock stroked
a place now we have both met,
face first with intimacy and grunting,
now I betray 3 times a day
in showers milking into a cupped hand,
slatting clean down the drain, scrubbing lost siblings away
with body wash and an AXE loofah.
My penis penetrated this delivery room
that fed you your mother's blood and breath,
fed you her muscle, her dark hair and deep eyes, and still
I betray your mother's entire landscape, thinking
of hitchhikers with tits and legs like neon arrows,
leading me by the tongue to a sweetness
of hips and lipstick. I beg to take back the deed,
the wet and heated deed that made you
present in this white room.
I'd wish you instead, as if joy and sweetness
don't come of carnal acts, of which love is made of loves
that are sick if mixed, but impossible to untwine.
Because sweetheart, life is a dirty puddle,
an ooze collecting residue, raw and moist,
and despite the unknowable behind you,
despite the delinquent training from gods and stars
with their "throw them in the deep end"
swimming instructions, know what hands
we land in are always a mixture
of liquids, sediments, and grace.

## Meditation on an Empty Stomach

If the stomach has a bottom
hunger does not
so at what point does the dark
become a universe
and we become planets
adrift in the carnivorous
cavernous depth
of our own want
how can we be stable
in a fractional moment of balance
stop fleeing, stop tugging
between now and then and when
can we take hold of the fruit and see
neither seed nor rot
see only the glistening red
see only the fuel-less fiery orange
and want neither to consume
nor to be devoured

## Baby Food

At 6 months my daughter attempts to eat a rocking chair,
and despite the ravaging cuteness of the scene she is but one
more mouth in a world of empty stomachs. But how many
hungers until we trip the threshold, slip all control and whimsy
and gobble down this planet like a ham hock to the bone?

Yet somehow, by her birth, we have Houdinied human life
out from the killing earth. And this seems significant, holy
really, as if god were a woman holding her ankles in the air
or as if I had some power to conjure from senseless questions,
which is what hunger is— a questioning of our blended flavors

in our first fixes of breast milk and pureed carrots, our first mouthfuls
of black raspberry ice cream and sips of scotch, or where our tongues
first taste each other, so close to that unknowable texture of love,
daring lover's teeth to eat us alive. Because hunger is forever
near perfect emptiness, nearly, like how love is nearly an act

of cannibalism, because we are all made up of each other
and the food of babies, who eat questions before milk—
who, like me, suck nipple to mouth as if breasts and rocking chairs
might explain the universe as she cries "let go and I will
eat the world, knowing it better than any with hands or eyes."

## Questions for Babies

Hey Baby,
Are you a peacock? An airplane, a planet or a song?
    Or will I kill such nonsense in you?
And what holds you inside? In place?
And what came first, the rhythm or the sound?
    The joy or the pain of its absence?
And was god in a box? Does he use you to get out?
    Is he trapped like a mouse in the drywall?
And what is the substance of space, this room that cradles the whole rigmarole?
And was the womb a wormhole?
    Were you the blip or the chance through the cosmic pinhole?
And is it easier at the beginning to remember where we came from?
And is the answer to true or false… yes?
And where do the objects go that are not permanent?
    Does love disappear when you can't see it?
And if I teach you the word for love, will I ruin it?
And what does the body feel like the first time you slip it on?
    Is the manual in another language altogether?
And what makes you not me, being made of me?
    What did you take from me that is missing?
Or Baby, are you the instant Nothing became hungry?
    Hungry, needing matter in mad gulps?
    Hungry, needing love like air needs a vacuum—
And is joy where we start feeling fed?

**On teaching my daughter proper nutrition**

The trick to marshmallows is to gorge
them into our mouths whole and puff
out our cheeks as if our teeth were bees.

But friendly bees. Buzz-buzz bees.
Teach us our alphabet and numbers bees.
giving grand speeches, mouths full,
letting gibberish drool from our cheeks

like marble-mouthed giants whose bellies
are never full, who fear hunger means dying,
calorie by calorie into a hole the size of a watch,

where gravity is a hungry universe
eagerly eating itself, where marshmallows
are digested, into an unknowable greatness.

So we must laugh, with marshmallows
stuffed between our teeth, and cling foolishly
to the hope we might take the bile out of being hungry

if only till the next nibble, eating sweets in cheek-fulls,
eating to keep running, running to keep from being eaten
by a hungry universe that gorges us into its mouth
whole.

## Meditation on an Empty Stomach

Hunger nags
until it's an entity
composed of fire
with no menus
I ate you instead
whom I hoped to love
chewed down to bones
got to know you by flavor
took you inside me
into the furnace
where I melt you down
into me
but to digest you
I must forget you
and lose you
in my appetite
and I learn of nothing
through the urges
of my stomach
and heart

**Still Life of a Candy Apple**

Shellacked fruit tastes better
for how we eat with our eyes
we need a stick to handle sweetness
and glue our fingers red
as if you could drink paint with a brush
drag sustenance out of canvas
taste honey-crisp or wine sap
dripping from food quivering in stillness
and the joy of nourishment
we can never digest

## A Playground Metaphor

We struggle
      like a see-saw
Love
      like tag
We fly
      like a swing
Pinned
      like a jungle-gym
We sing
      like blacktop—
Then retreat
      like recess

## Meditation on an Empty Stomach

I took a knife to the gut
hollowed out to the spine
plated the remains
as if reading tea leaves
for the food of my past
inside it all I found
the space of the house of me
then took the scalpel deeper
dissecting the empty parts
the spaces the nothingness
as if there was something hallowed
primordial and divine
desperate and silenced
singing the molecules of god
in the gaps we keep
but now the pieces squirm
free, wriggle and writhe
scatter and are gone
hopeless to be stitched
back whole

## Falling Asleep to Berryman and my Daughter's Lullaby

These toys have teeth
and we bail them over the side
in buckets. Buckets!

And did I say teeth?
Two rows and mean eyes
rain from sky
chewing on air
like a ventriloquist's dummy.

You gave them a taste, dear Bones,
      for human flesh
when you tickled little plastic insides
with every echo from the vast empty wanting.

So, Mr. Bones,
What do they dance when they leave?
What do they know when they go?

## Stranger Danger

> *"Come inside, it's fun inside!"*
> —Mickey Mouse Clubhouse Theme Song

sings this mouse, who's built a clubhouse
out of a giant corpse of himself,
his house, half-a-gorged head
planted in the flower bed,
feet tall as trees turned garage for mouse-shaped cars.
Everything is himself, names everything a "mouseketool"
the cakes he eats are made of his ears,
his girlfriend is him in a skirt,
and only the duck calls him
on this violent narcissism.
But even Donald sings his praises
for friendship and triangles and numbers
with enthusiasm worthy of a Branch Davidian
because Kool-Aid is a kid's drink
and all these kid's shows use the same lines
as a stranger with candy and an unmarked van,
where a mouse can act like he knows us
and knows our children and their love
of colors and high-pitched voices,
Hot-Dog dancing his way into our hearts
like a clog, singing
the beating of our own pulse
till his voice is indistinguishable from the murmur.

## The End of Play

Her games have no rhyme,
no reason, just a spectacle
of recklessness and open space.
She holds *wu,* smiling
in the way blocks become drums,
in the way she refuses to learn
the order of colors, numbers and letters,
in the way she conquers the universe
despite us, by cutting it loose and free.
And after, for the sake of security,
I close her windows shut,
collect the toys in a plastic chest,
collect the madness back
into stacks on bookshelves,
erase her Pollack maker scribbles
from the wall, and teach her to sleep
in a smaller, darker room.

## Meditation on an Empty Stomach

Empty stomach
ready to eat
never spoiled
ready to fill
already full
already knowing
ready to digest—
it is the space
that holds
everything
we are
It is the space
that holds
what we have lost

**Parental Advice**

Tell your baby this:

You have no eyes,
don't look with your eyes.

You have no ears,
don't hear with your ears.

You have no nose,
all smells are yours.

You have no skin,
feel no inside or out.

And don't taste with your tongue,
know the world with no mouth.

Because babies were not meant to be in pieces.
    and maybe they can take in the entire world,
    remembering what we forgot,
    with their whole body at once.

**Practice to Write**

> *A Vietnamese children's paintings, "Practice to Write" depicts a tired mother sitting at a kitchen table while her young child, painted with no hands, attempts to learn to write using her mouth.*

There are no names to your drawing,
so I slip and call you Ariadne, my daughter,
and see her with no hands.

An adult's voice falls short.
The mother, yours or hers,
has fallen heavy—"The baby has thrown up again."

I slip and call her Adrienne, my wife,
while I muse on my own death,
and die like my father,

without grace or plot,
without war or ditch.
And I am selfish to make this about me,

which is itself an act of war,
painting pictures of my own
death overtop of yours, leaving nothing

but the heat and sick sugar
that stings with sweetness
like a candy grenade.

And you, or is it Ariadne,
are writing to fill the blank spaces
of her hands, the pencil in her mouth,

as if learning were an act
of devouring.
So I am selfish,

this is about me, or the lack of me
hiding outside the corners,
watching all that you have drawn.

## Explaining Bombs to Babies

I threw a bomb
        to keep myself from running
                away

I threw a bomb
        into a school yard
        to detonate their alpha
            -bet, the shrapnel spells
                  "Fuck you! I'm standing here,

      Next to you!"

I threw a bomb in church
        to see God in a shock
        -wave, to see his work
            pixelated and subatomic

I threw a bomb to merge us together
            in an irrevocable and permanent violence,
stained in sprayed blood and blended sinew

      A bomb to see you from the inside
                            out
A bomb so I can be everywhere at once
        in an instant
eternal,
        to have eyes of shrapnel

I threw a bomb to make space,
        a bomb to break
                  sound and silence,
      a bomb
            to fuck      my enemies,
            A bomb to no joy so sweet that the tears
    I weep are concussive

I threw a bomb to teach the world mercy


And Baby, I will fill the world with bombs
      for you
        until a single bomb is
                as loud
as a prayer

      in a crowded room.

## Colic

Because there is no word for hunger good enough to feed you
Because you can't just float but your body is a fish
    on a beach
    at noon
    in a tourniquet and needs to nurse
Because growing teeth is the mouth eating itself
Because gravity is the mouth of the Earth
Because the Earth is a womb like a shark is a pet
Because a question is the size of the moon
    when you wear it in your skin
    when crying can't ask it
Because you know sadness as a hunger for a past present with nothingness
Because you know sadness as a hunger for a future present with nothingness
Because the Earth is a womb like high school is a hug
Because you know love without metaphor
    like sunlight
    like restless weather
Because you can see I will teach you the word for loss
And even then, you will still scream primitive into the maw of creation

## Baby Talk

This is a poem about gibberish
and it is already ruined.

I want to shake a nursery rhyme
and read only the words that fall out,
those loose tooth words
that can't stand the crowd of the mouth.

Because any word small enough
to fit in our mouths
is small enough to choke on.

And choking has more meaning than words,
we get no breath,
we get the silence
we try to mash up and chew.

With mouths we mangle hot noise,
the cruel device that turns sound ignorant,
drains it of its truth and vibration.

This is a poem about gibberish,
which is the surrender of hope
that by the end
any of this will be any clearer.

**Learning to Cook**

You have to let that jazz sizzle,
let it crackle and hiss in the oil
like angry rain, and smoke sweet and burnt
and reckless. Because you need to cook
like you want to eat,
with juicy cinnamon fingers,
shoveling the meal like a person searching
for the core of the Earth,
with ravenous spittle leaking from their lips,
drunk between the flavor and the texture,
between the dream and the meat.
Because in eating we remember we are primal,
hungry and made of the food of wild beasts
who taste with the whole body
flavors we ruin cooking from recipes.

## Meditation on an Empty Stomach

The baby passed
from your belly, now softer,
and she cries as if she knows
this cradle will rock then fall
that's what we sing to her
so she can feel her own frailty
feel her pulse and mistake it for a leak
the way water drains from a stream
into the ocean, the nameless origin
we mistake for the nameless forever
of feedings to stave off hunger
as if it were the sorrow of us
staring into the cosmic swallowing
screaming with our whole being
at planets and the gravity that holds
us against them
keeping us from the void
that spins asunder in the black—
yet despite us she breathes
so I will take her lead and smile
and if by the grace of our dying
we find the quality of our life
may I go screaming and weeping
with sweaty fists and rage
dragged into the ending
I share with you
all

## My Gratitude

The author would like to take this time to thank some very important people, without whom this book would not be possible:

First and foremost, my partner Adrienne, without whom there would be no poet here to write these poems, and whose love, brilliance, and strength inspired so much of this book.

Next to my mentors and finders of wayward souls (my own included): A nod to Richard Madigan, Bill Broun, and Kim McKay for early support and guidance down a scary path. To Patrick Rosal for a swift and needed jarring of reality. To Alicia Ostriker for teaching me to write my fears. To Ross Gay for teaching me to let go. To Ellen Dore-Watson for a calming presence in some very chaotic waters, both within my writing and beyond. And at last, in ever-enduring memory and thanks to Jane Mead for such brilliant feedback and support. Rest in peace dear poet.

And to a list of readers and colleagues whose helped me discover more and more of myself with each brilliant interpretation of my work in its struggling, embryotic stages: Michelle Greco, Shaun Fletcher, Jesse Burns, Roberto Carlos Garcia, Elliott batTzedek, Tara Yetter, Jude-Laure Denis, Mary Brancaccio, Darla Himeles, Yesenia Montilla, Cara Armstrong, Rick Carter, Freya Mercer, Sosha Pinson, Mathew Klitsch, Jane Seitel, Ysabel Y. Gonzalez, Daniel McLaughlin, Thomas Krivak, and Fadel K. Jabr. Also, a million gifts of gratitude to those who helped me in more real-world ways, without which I would not have been able to publish this book: Theresa Pratt, Kevin Hayes, Eric Smith, and Brandon Gilbert.

And finally, more thanks than words or books could possibly return: To Jennifer Young— Payment in full.

Michael Lee Bross was born in July of 1977, a child of the disco and Star Wars era. He was raised in Wantage, New Jersey, in the shadow of High Point State Park and grew up a lover of fantasy, science fiction, music, mythology, and nearly all aspects of the written word. During his formative years, Michael was deeply affected by the death of his father, who was a victim of the HIV epidemic that struck during the tail end of the 20th century.

Before returning to school in his late twenties, Michael worked within a number of different careers: as a professional actor and stagehand, a bartender/waiter, a nurse's aide in developmental disability and brain trauma clinics, even a secretary for a children's sock company, but writing and poetry were an always present and guiding force in his life. Early on he found solace and inspirations in the works of Gary Snyder, Kurt Vonnegut, Ray Bradbury, Ursula LeGuin, Campbell McGrath, and Dean Young, to name just a few.

Michael's poetry is an examination of recklessness and spontaneity. He is fascinated by the catalytic power of language and its ability to push the boundaries of not only thought but experience as well. His approach is geared towards discovery, which at times leads him to the sincere, whilst other times to the odd and delightful. At the center of his work lies the driving force of questioning and introspection, holding more interest in the pursuit than the final destination.

He is a graduate of the MFA in Poetry program at Drew University, and is an active writer of both poetry and fiction. He is the recipient of the Martha E. Martin Awards for Poetry and Fiction, as well as the Jane Coil Cole Poetry Scholarship and the 2015 Arts by the People Chapbook Award. His work has been published in such periodicals as *Lifeboat, Mobius Poetry Magazine,* and *Let's Talk Philadelphia.*

Michael lives in North Eastern Pennsylvania, where he resides with his partner, Adrienne, and their daughter, Ariadne. He currently teaches Composition and English at the University of Scranton, East Stroudsburg University, and Centenary University in New Jersey. He is also the lead editor for *D10again*, an internet platform for tabletop gaming journalism. Michael is currently working on his follow up poetry collection, a speculative fiction novel, and a community outreach program featuring creative writing and tabletop roleplaying games.

www.ingramcontent.com/pod-product-compliance
Lightning Source LLC
LaVergne TN
LVHW040118080426
835507LV00041B/1615